Where in the World Would You Go Today?

Written by Cynthia Belnap   Illustrated by Jaimee Christensen

Where in the world would you go today?
What would you like to see?

There are so many places to visit,
It is hard to decide, I agree!

Would you go to the hot, dry desert
and walk through the sand in the sun?

Would you sit in the shade of a cactus
and watch the small lizards run?

Would you go to the wet, salty ocean
and swim in the water so deep?

Would you ride on the waves when it's windy and watch the gray dolphins leap?

Would you hike up a rocky, steep mountain, up high where the trees don't grow?

Would you sit on a rock, like an eagle,
and look at the valley below?

Would you visit the green rainforest
with monkeys in trees up high?

Would you rest by the edge of a river
and watch all the bright birds fly?

Where in the world would you go today?
What would you like to see?
Anywhere that you went in the world
would be a great place to be!